Poems for the one you love

POEMS FOR THE ONE YOU LOVE

*Tell the one you love
just how much they mean.*

WILLIAM MCKAY

XULON PRESS

Xulon Press
2301 Lucien Way #415
Maitland, FL 32751
407.339.4217

www.xulonpress.com

Printed in the United States of America

Paperback ISBN-13: 978-1-6628-4202-3
Ebook ISBN-13: 978-1-6628-4203-0

You have a smile I had to see.
I knew that it, just wasn't me.
You had a smile that made me care.
You made me feel, that is not fair.
I know that I'd been hurt before.
But your smile I do adore.
I knew I had to let you in.
So, something special could begin.
A new beginning it would be.
Me for you and you for me.

About commitments that we make.
Some we keep and some we break.
With commitments please be true.
Try to be a better you.
I try to be a better me.
To be the best that I can be.
Do all things you swore you would.
Just keep them if you could.
Keep your word as best you can.

I Try to be the better man.
This also goes for women to.
You must be the better you.
If they broke their vows to you?
Do what's ever best to do.
You deserve someone who's true.
In turn you must be true too.

I used to long for yesterday.
But that was long ago.
Today I seek tomorrow.
So, I am not alone.
I have found the one for me.
soon together we will be.
I can't be with you yet today.
When I do, I'll be ok.
I kept searching high and low.
How I found you, I don't know.
I'm not alone, I do foresee
It is now both you and me.
We know a couple we must be.
I know that I have found you though.
And by her smile I think she knows.
That you and I are meant to be.
Together we'll live happily.

It's with the pen our thoughts are heard.
Heard in letters not in words.
The pen does speak but silently.
Its words we read not verbally.
It says a story to be sure.
Sometimes it's wicked others pure.
So, I ask you read with care.
To know the truth, you must be fair.

When I was young, I thought I knew my way.
But in my life, it seems That trouble came to stay.
Then a special woman Finally came my way.
I have a feeling you're the one I've been looking for.
your smile makes me feel a way I've seldom
felt before.
I saw you the first time when I walked into your store.
The only thing I knew right then, I wanted
you for sure.
And the way I felt for you was absolutely pure.
Now that I have found you here.
there's something you should know.
I'm not going anywhere unless you say to go.

I want to know you oh so well.
Who you are I can't quite tell?
I think you're a good person though.
I can't quite Say just how I know.
You have a smile that warms my heart.
I wish, of your life to be a part.

I want you with me every day.
To know you love me in that way.
In the way that lovers do.
To think I mean that much to you.
Just to have you in my life.
To think one day, you'll be my wife.
This is what I want with you.
Just to know you love me too.
There's nothing that I'd rather do.
Then know that I am loved by you.

In the morning right at dawn.
I can't sleep because your gone.
In my mind I see you here.
What I'd give to have you near.
I await, for your return.
In my heart the candle burns.
When I have you here again.
I'll show you that I love you then.

Now I have you here with me
You are the only one I see.
When you smile it warms my heart?
For of my life, you are a part.
When you look at me and frown.
Nothing gets me farther down.
If I can make you smile for me.
No greater joy is there to me.

I love it when I see you smile.
It makes me happy quite a while.
When it is you that makes me smile.
I know I'll go the extra mile.
To see you swank and dressed in style.
I've wanted for a great long while.
To make you happy don't you see.
That is what I want for me.

You have a smile so soft and sweet.
When I'm with you I feel complete.
Now I'm here to speak to you.
You make me feel the way I do.
You have a heart, and it beats true.
All I know is I want you.
Will you now go out with me?
I'll be the best that I can be.

When I saw your lovely smile.
Pretty eyes all dressed in style.
You have a softness I could see.
I want to see you smile for me.
When I saw your smile again.
I knew I had to have you then.

I always thought that it was me.
All because, I could not see.
I could not see, the truth in you.
I did not know what I should do.
Now I know I'll love again.
And I know what I'll do then.
I'll find someone to give my heart.
And of her life then be a part.

I've searched the country over.
Then I found you here.
When I looked into your eyes.
It got very clear.
You are the one I searched for.
All these lonely years.
Now that I have found you.
I haven't any fear.
I just have one thing to say.
And I'll be very clear.
You are the only one I want.
You see I love you dear.

I have searched for just that special way.
To tell you how I feel.
A way to let you know.
My love for you is real.
The words just seem to slip away.
Every time I try.
The only thing I'm certain of.
I do not know just why.
just know dear that I love you.
in so many ways.
I just know I love you more.
with every passing day.

I wrote this just for you, my love.
To tell you that I care.
I just think that you and me.
Make the perfect pair.
What I want to know from you.
Is that you too do care.
If you do, it can be said.
That life is truly fair.

I am so glad I have you.
That you are in my life.
What I wish to tell you.
I do with tempered fright.
I don't just want you in my life.
I want you for my wife.
tell me you will have me.
and I'll know great delight.

I chose these words to tell you.
Just how much I care.
I could not wait till you get home.
I had no time to spare.
I had to say I love you.
To hold you through the day.
Again, I say I love you.
Because I feel that way.

I look forward to when you are here.
I won't want nor will I feel fear.
I look to when we will be one.
Two distinct together one.

I don't know what your life's been.
I know together we will win.
One and one make three.
First there's you then there's me.
You and me and we make three.

I wait for the day to come.
To learn about where you come from.
I want to know how your lives been.
We can change the now not then.
We'll decide what is to be.
We'll do so as both you and me.
I only know what my life's been.
You made me fall in love again.

I'll stay with you if you allow.
I'll show you I will break no vow.
Know this that my heart beats true.
That my heart belongs to you.
It's true what I say today.
Everything will be ok.

Deep within my heart you dwell.
I'm not one to kiss and tell.
But for you in love I fell.
See now what you are to me.
Everything that you should be.
I want you for all my life.
Will you please become my wife?

Every time I think of you.
It always makes me smile too.
I think of when I'll have you here.
Of when at last, I'll have you near.
I'll say I love you twice a day.
I only ask don't walk away.
Tell me that you're going to stay.
Then everything will be ok.

I do love you can't you tell.
For upon your smile, I dwell.
There's nothing that I'd rather see.
Then to have you smile at me.
There's nothing that I'd rather hear.
Then hear you say I love you dear.

When I'm with you I can see.
The road that lay ahead of me.
It's a road that's full of joy.
Just don't treat me like a toy.
To you my love I did sell.
If you accept, I will do well.
I ask for your love, you have mine.
If you do this, we'll both be fine.

I do love you and it is true.
I want no one else but you.
I hope and pray you love me too.
If you, do it can be said.
I feel cheer instead of dread.
I will as long, as I have you.
As long dear, as you want me too.

If you love me, like I love you.
You will always want me too.
We'll be together you and me.
I believe it's destiny.

Know this that my love is true.
That I am in love with you.
Tell me that you love me too.
Here me now. To you I tell.
It is within my heart you dwell.

I'll love you till the end of time.
If you declare that your mine.
I'll be with you if you see.
You are the only one for me.
I tell you now so please hear.
You're the one that I love dear.

Together we will be as one.
Along the way we'll have some fun.
I say now this much is true.
That I am in love with you.
I just want to have you here.
So, I can hold you close my dear.
This is what I want from you.
To be the better half of two.
Because my dear I do love you.

I knew it when I saw you.
I had to make you mine.
I did not know just what to do.
To find a way to make you see.
You'll be happy here with me.
Together we will build our lives.
Together we will have some fun.
We'll also have some work to do.
That never will be done.
The only thing, I want to ask.
with me will you come.

I want to hold you tight my dear.
Every day now that you're here.
I always want to have you near.
The only thing that I now fear.
Are you'll get tired of being here?

Now my darling that you're here.
I just want to hold you near.
To have your body next to mine.
A dream come true that is divine.
I'll hold you with great delight.
And everything will be alright.

I'll find a way to make you love me.
I'll try every day.
I will keep on trying.
Till I find a way.
I won't just let it be.
I'll try my best to keep your heart.
Showing you each day.
I won't take you for granted.
I'll let you know each day.
That I really love you.
In that special way.
I want to hold you in my arms.
That is what I want to do.
I want to hold you all day long.
Because dear I love you.

I want to show I love you.
Each and every day.
And I want to show you.
In a special way.
I'll say the things you need to hear.
Every chance I get.
I will find a way.
So, you don't feel regret.
For being here with me.
I'll make sure we live our lives.
And do so happily.

I'll tell you that I love you.
Several times a day.
When I wake up in the morning.
That is how I'll start the day.
Then again at bedtime too.
But those are not the only times.
That I'll say I love you.

You have a smile I love to see.
Because it warms my heart.
I just want you in my life.
To be a major part.
You have a lovely smile.
tell me that it's true.
is the smile just a front?
or is it really you.

Yes, I truly want you.
I want you every day.
The only thing that scares me.
Is will you walk away.
Yes, my dear I want you.
Do you want me too?
If you do, there is something left to say.
I think I love you more and more.
With every passing day.

I'm waiting till you get here.
You see I count the days.
When you finally get here.
Will you stay or walk away.
Will you want to keep me?
Or find another way.
I tell you that I want you.
I'll show you in some way.
I'll show you that I love you.
In that special way.

You have a smile that drew me in.
I knew that I found love again.
I didn't think to question why.
I just want you by my side.
I had to have you this is true.
Because I am in love with you.

I knew it when I saw you.
I had to make you mine.
I said I'd find a way my dear.
a way to get you here.
I had to have you with me.
I knew it had to be.
I'll give you the best of me.
Hoping you will see.
The present that I give you.
The man inside that's me.

When time comes around.
That it's love that I have found.
That's when you get here.
My heart will fill with cheer.
Then everything will be all right.
The day that I can hold you tight.

I will wait to look upon your smile.
For you I'll go the extra mile.
I want you in this place.
With a smile upon your face.
Now that you are here with me.
I'll be as happy as can be.

What I'd give to have you here.
So, I could belay your fear.
There's no need to fear from me.
I'm a gentle man you see.
I'll be with you all the time.
Yet I know that you're not mine.
I'll be with you in my mind.
You are your own girl this I see.
Won't you share your life with me.

I know when you smile at me.
It makes me as happy as can be.
I so want to hold you tight.
So, I know it will be right.
Just to take a walk with you.
Would be for me a dream come true.

I wish to take a walk with you.
When you get here.
that's what we will do.
When we do, I'll hold your hand.
To let you know I am your man.
I wish to spend my life with you.
I hope and pray you want me too.

To hold your body next to mine.
Is a dream come true of mine.
If I can hold you every day.
Everything will be ok.

When I saw you with your lovely smile.
Standing there all dressed in style.
I knew I'd go the extra mile.
Just to hold you for a while.

I can't wait till you get here.
Because right now I'm full of fear.
When you get here then we will see.
If you and I are meant to be.
I think now that we will see.
I think it is meant to be.

Now dear that I have you.
I'm not sure what to do.
First thing let me start by saying.
Baby I love you.
I want you here with me.
As much as you can stand to be.
I'll always love you baby.
But honey that's just me.

Early in the morning.
You're the first thing that I see.
Then I smile from ear to ear.
Because you're still with me.
When I lay down in the evening.
You re the last sight that I see.
I know that in the morning.
You'll wake up with me.

Skin so fair yet coal black hair.
Your sweet smile just isn't fair.
you reached in and grabbed my heart.
you captured me right from the start.
I had to see you smile for me.
I just knew that this must be.
If we're together, we'll do well.
Because with you in love I fell.

All day long I think of you.
Sometimes the only thing I do.
I can see you smile you see.
I want to see you smile for me.
Sometimes I wonder can this be.
When I see you smile at me?
I'll know if it's meant to be.
Is there to be a you and me.
I truly hope that this will be.

Listen close my darling.
Only you will do.
No one out there loves me.
Quite the way you do.
That's just fine by me my dear.
All my love is here.
And it all belongs to you.

I do love you sweetheart.
Oh, so very much.
So much so my darling.
I long to feel your touch.
When I can hold you every day.
Everything will be ok.
I'll accept it come what may.
And wear a smile every day.
For as long as you're ok.

Come and see me now my dear.
I'll be better once you're here.
when I can hold you tight.
And look at you to say good night.
I will also say I love you.
And hope you say you love me too.
when I wake up next to you.
I'll know you love me too.

I do want to feel your touch.
In fact, I want it very much.
When I can feel you next to me.
Oh, so happy I will be.

Every day seems longer.
That you are away.
Perhaps because I miss you more.
With every passing day.
I want to hold you darling.
In my arms embrace.
Know this that I want you.
My space belongs to you.
Come walk through life with me.
I know we'll do so happily.

I want you in every way.
I want you more with every day.
Tell me that you want me too.
That you love me like I love you.
That is what I want from you.
Nothing short of love will do.
Because I'm so in love with you.

Soon you will be here with me.
We'll be together you and me.
Then my dear we will see.
If you can stand to be with me.
If you can then it will be.
we will be two or maybe three.
We'll just have to wait and see.

I am here and you are there.
You do not know how much I care.
I just want you here with me.
So together we can be.
It always will be you and me.
Though we may add one, two or three.
Then a family we will be.

I was lonely then you came.
I was tired of playing games.
I want a girl that feels the same.
It's true that I've been hurt before.
She won't hurt me anymore.
I believe your heart I pure.
This I feel I know for sure.

In the future I can see.
A life is there for you and me.
And together we will be.
A loving couple maybe three.
We'll have our small family.
That's what's ahead for you and me.

Soon you will be here with me.
Then together we will be.
We will build a future you and me.
I will not ask or reason why.
The future is ours to build and form.
Or from my arms you will be torn.
If we're here for us, you see.
Together happy we will be.

You say you're happy then I smile.
For more than just a little while.
It makes me happy don't you see.
That you're smiling just for me.
I think I'll make you smile some more.
It's a pleasure not a chore.
I could not wait till you got home.
You're in my life I'm not alone.
I am by myself just me.
I'm really, not alone you see.
Tonight, you will come home to me.
And then happy I will be.

I love you more than words can say.
More than grammar can convey.
I love you in a special way.
I love you and I want you here.
I want to hold close my dear.

I long to have you by my side.
I love you much and I know why.
You are a special girl that's true.
I am so in love with you.
Just to have you here with me.
means I will live happily.

you are so special you don't see.
just how much you mean to me.
I know love because of you.
That's just one thing that you do.
Through you darling I can see.
Light that lies inside of me.
With you it sees light of day.
And everything is then ok.

I'm so glad that you are here.
To softly whisper in my ear.
To hold your body next to me.
is a dream come true for me?
Only now that you are here.
That the future's coming clear.
I am so glad that you are here.
As the days go rolling past.
They seem to go, so very fast.
I want to spend my days with you.
I guess for now the nights will do
as for now I bide my time.
at least for now I know your mine.

listen close to what I say.
it's not games, I wish to play.
I have come today to talk with you.
To tell you how I feel for you.
I want to say my love is true.
I wish to spend my life with you.

Won't you come and stay with me.
I'll make you happy wait and see.
If you will give me a chance.
I'll find a way to make you dance.
I just want to make you smile.
If you'll sit with me a little while.
I want you to be with me.
Say that you will stay with me.

you make me smile every day.
things just seem to go my way.
let me be in love with you.
you'll find out what I can do.
If you will only love me too.

this I will do every day.
with you is where I choose to stay.
I'll make you smile in many ways.
If you choose to let me stay.
I will never walk away.
I'll gladly stay with you for life.
If you choose to be my wife.

If only I could show you all my love for you.
You wouldn't have to question everything I do.
Know this that my love is all for you.
I do not want another, that is something I can't do.
Though my love is plentiful it all belongs to you.
Yes, my dear my heart is pure my love is all for you.
You see I just can't help it I am so in love with you.

I want you with me every day.
If you are, I'll be, ok?
If you want to be with me.
I would live life happily.
What I really want to say.
I love you more with every day.
Together we will be ok.

I want you now, I'm true to heart.
I know that now we are apart.
Could it be that you and me?
Could someday a couple be.
If it is let me know?
My love for you I then will show.

If I succeed and make you mine.
I know then I will be fine.
I'll take some time and we will see.
We Will create a you and me.
And together we will be.

In the day when you're at work.
I feel like being such a jerk.
It's just I'm lost when your away.
Because your gone most every day.
That is why I have to say.
I just can't stand when you're away.
I wait all day for your return.
For your touch I sit and yearn.

I pass the time when your away.
But you must know I'm not ok.
I write my words to pass the time.
But I'm not good while you're away.
And you're gone most every day.
I always smile when you arrive.
It is then I feel alive.

Time is all I have that's mine.
it passes once for its last time.
it's what I have that I can share.
yet I have no time to spare.
I choose to spend my time with you.
It's really all I want to do.
When I say that I love you.
Know this that my love is true.
Now I want you here with me.
I hope soon that this will be.
Know I want to be with you.
There's nothing I would rather do.

Your smile so soft and sweet.
I knew at once that we would meet.
But I was here, and you were there.
But no one said that life was fair.
Now that you are finally here.
I wish to hold you close my dear.
There is one vow I make to you.
I love you now and will be true.
I'll always be in love with you.

You have a smile that won my heart.
Yet of my life you're not a part.
I ask you now to speak to me.
Perhaps a couple we can be.
If only, you'll go out with me.

Time has come for us to meet.
I tell you now your heart I seek.
I'll try to win your heart today.
I hope that things do go ok.
Take some time and speak with me.
I do like you do you like me.
I truly hope that this can be.
I hope that you'll go out with me.

Tell me that you feel it too.
That you love me as I love you.
I know you're special this is true.
That is the reason I love you.
Every time you look at me.
There is a special smile I see.
It's ok I smile too.
Every time I look at you.

I didn't know what you meant to me.
Or how important you could be.
When you came into my life.
I wanted you to be my wife.
The only thing that I could tell.
Is that I am under your sweet spell.
I knew that it just had to be.
You are the one that's meant for me.

Now I have you here with me.
There is a future I can see.
One with you to be with me.
I know together we should be.
In a place for you and me.
We'll write our own destiny.

I've walked through life a lonely heart.
I was of nothing then a part.
It seemed that nowhere I belonged.
I've learned now that I was wrong.
I found a place that's meant for me.
A place for you as well as me.
I found a place where I belong.
I knew at once I was not wrong.
I now live life quite happily.
For I have you to walk with me.

When I saw you smile at me?
I knew at once that we must be.
That together we would do well.
That to you myself I'd sell.
I knew I'd have you here with me.
And that together we would be.

You have a smile I can't resist.
It wasn't one I could dismiss.
It reached in and grabbed my heart.
To of your life become a part.
Is really what I want to start.
I knew together we must be.
A place to live for you and me.
Please my dear just let it be.
I'll be for you if you're for me.

Surely there will be we.
When you choose to walk with me.
I learned how happy I can be.
just because you smile at me.
tell me how to win your heart.
and of your life become a part.

the time has come but not yet passed.
for us to be as one at last.
to make an us, both you and me.
and that together we should be.
learn to give as well as take.
and know our love is no mistake.
for you to give us both a brake.
that is what our love will take.

I can see your smile so well.
You spoke my name your voice trailed.
You had a smile that touched my heart.
Though of my life you weren't a part.
I wanted you this you could see.
If you would just go out with me
I said I loved you this is true.
It's true I love no one, but you.
just to have you here with me.
I will give the best of me.
If I could just be here with you.
I'd give my very best to you.
If I could have you by my side.
I wouldn't run I wouldn't hide.

I have waited many years.
But not with joy and not with cheer.
But I say you're worth the wait.
You didn't come early.
You didn't come late.
But right on time for our first date.

I was sad and lonely.
You see I walked alone.
You see I had nobody.
I could call my own.
I learned to do so many things.
Mostly on my own.
One thing I could not teach myself.
Was not to be alone.
You must have a teacher.
To learn to be a part.
You can't even teach yourself.
if you're true to heart.
someone just must let you.
of their life become a part.

You brought me joy and happiness.
You also brought me love.
You came not like hawk.
But rather like a dove.
As if you came on angels' wings.
You came from up above.

I knew it when I saw you there.
Gorgeous smile and lovely hair.
I know I had to have you.
To whom to give my love.
I knew the way you smiled.
When you spoke my name.
I could see you liked me too.
And that you felt the same.

if I could only make you smile.
I'd gladly go the extra mile.
If I could make you smile for me.
Oh, how happy I would be.
To think that I'm the reason why.
Would make me a happy guy.

If I could give you reason.
To want to wear a smile.
I would have my head held high.
And you would be the reason why.
I would even close my eyes.
And see you smile again.
I could truly say that I'd be happy then.

Just to hold you in my arms.
Would prove I do indeed have charm.
What I feel when you're with me.
How much more lucky can I be.
Then I am when you're with me.

Now I Have you in my life.
I now want you to be my wife.
Tell me that you want me too.
I'll show you then what I can do.
I can do well many things.
You'll find out I even sing.

If I had, you in my life.
I'd wait until you are my wife.
I would not care how long it takes.
I wouldn't wish to make mistakes.
I just want to be with you.
That's really all I want to do.

The morning that I came to you.
I didn't know what I would do.
I just want to ask you out.
I must admit I have my doubts.
So will you please go out with me.
I'll be so happy you want me.

Now dear that I have you here.
I won't feel sad I won't feel fear.
I'm just glad to have you near.
Won't you be with me tonight.
If you, will I'll feel delight.
I just want to be with you.
There's nothing I would rather do.

Come away with me today.
It's my treat I'll gladly pay.
I just want to be with you.
You can say what we will do.
If I can be with you.

On my journey I found you.
I knew right then what I must do.
I'll find a way to talk to you.
I want to show you that I care.
I even bought these clothes to wear.
And brought to you to tailor fit.
To make you smile and that's not it.
I really want to take you out.
That's what this is all about.

Yes, I knew that you were here.
I came today to see you dear.
Could there be a you and me?
Perhaps a couple we could be.
If you will just go out with me.
Perhaps then happy we'll both be.

I'm asking please go out with me.
And we can see then what will be.
if you like me and I like you.
We can see then what we'll do.

I've known sorrow I've known strife.
All's good now you're in my life.
I can't express how great I feel.
Now you're here and it's for real.

I'm in want of something new.
I have it now because it's you.
I hope you wish to be with me.
If you wish to pleasure me.
Just say that you're in love with me.
Oh, how happy I would be.

Time will tell us that's for sure.
If what we have is strong and pure.
They will test you this is true.
Perhaps they'll meet a stronger you.
They'll try to drive us far apart.
Please try to keep me in your heart.
We can handle what they give.
I now exist, with you I'll live.

To feel I am the reason.
For the smile upon your face.
Like if I could have you Living in my place.
Then my place would be our home.
I Would not walk the world alone.
I could wear a smile too.
All because I now have you.

I saw a smile upon your face.
I lost my words I lost my place.
I can close my eyes and see you smile again.
I will always want you then.
It always makes me smile too.
The reason is that I have you.
Know this that I love you dear.
I want to make that very clear.

I write to you with great delight.
To reach your heart try as I might.
I want to reach you here tonight.
You came far to be with me.
I want to make you happy see.
To make you wish to stay with me.
That a couple we should be.
That's really what you want for me.

To be a couple two as one.
To show you dear where I come from.
The life I Knew was hard and bleak.
But one day I knew we'd meet.
You brought joy into my life.
I ask you now to be my wife.

You are the one I looked for.
For so very long.
I think I finally found a place.
Right where I belong.
I think my place is by your side.
With you all the way.
There is no place I'd rather be.
A heavy price I paid.

You have a smile so lovely.
It reaches out to me.
It reaches out and grabs my heart.
And gets the best of me.
I just know I'll do my part.
To bring you close to me.
Because I think together.
We will make history see.

You have a lovely smile that true.
It's lovely just because it's you.
It brings joy into my heart.
That of my life you play a part.
just to get good praise from you.
is really what I want to do.
you have a charm that I can see.
it makes you a part of me.
your touch is warm your eyes are clear.
please tell me that you want me here.

Yes, I wondered can it be.
do you have a thing for me?
can it be I hope it is.
that we have our love that is.
do we share a love that's true?
that you love me like I love you.
will we walk through life as one?
tell me that we are not done.
but that our hearts now beat as one.

tell me that it's meant to be.
there is to be a you and me.
tell me as we're standing here.
in more than space that we are near.
that even we are apart.
your still with me in my heart.
when we're together don't you see.
I'll always give the best of me.

I wish every day you could feel the way I feel.
Then you would know beyond a doubt.
my love for you is real.
I love you with all my heart.
I only fear one day we'll part.
So, promise you will stay with me.
And that together we will be.

The day will come that it will pass.
And we will be as one at last.
There will be a you and me.
And together we will be.
If we are both alive.
A love like ours is bound to thrive.

If I, have you by my side?
I will not ask or reason why.
As long, as you are here with me.
A loving couple we will be.
Today and always you and me.

I love you more than I can say.
Much more than grammar can convey.
I love you more with every day.
I love you in so many ways.
I know I love you this is true.
I'll always be in love with you.

Every day we are apart.
Another arrow in my heart.
The way I feel when you're not here.
Another day that I feel fear.
Because you are not here with me.
I spend each day in misery.
But when I have you here with me.
I am as happy as can be.

In the day when you're not home.
I am here and all alone.
Time goes slow when you are not here.
That is because I love you dear.
Now your home and all is good.
I've even fixed you up some food.
I just want you here with me.
Perhaps then happy I can be.

You can scour the world you see.
You'll never find another me.
I'm not who you thought I was.
Your haunted by the memories.
of the one that wasn't me.
You can't forget though just because.
Or let go of what never was.
I was always there for you.
Know me then or will that do.
Try to be the better you.
And know that I am better too.

Can you take me as I am.
The truth is I'm a real good man.
I'm better than you thought of me.
Now you know the real true me.
Is it really me you, see?
Or the man you thought I was.
Isn't really, just because.
The thing my dear you didn't see.
The person you once thought was me.
Was someone I could never be.

Tell me darling who am I?
Can I be your special guy?
I can't see what is to be.
Am I for you are you for me?
Tell me it is meant to be.
That you wish to be with me.
Because I want to be with you.
But I don't know just what to do.
except to say that I love you.

I've come to see you here today.
I'm hoping things will go my way.
And then you'll say you're here to stay.
I want to take you out with me.
If you will go out with me.
I'll make you happy wait and see.
The least you'll get is a good dinner.
We hit it off we'll both be winners.

It seems that your too lovely.
For a man like me.
You could have much better.
But you still wanted me.
Yes, I sometimes wonder.
Just how that could be.
How someone so special.
Could love a man like me.

One thing that I know is true.
I just want to be with you.
I hope that you want me too.
It is you I do adore.
I just want you even more.

I wish that I could be with you.
Every single day.
Tell me that you want that too.
I want to say I love you.
Everything will be ok.
I want to lay down next to you.
Then wake up that way.

Every time I see you.
My feelings grow so strong.
And I know deep in my heart.
My feelings can't be wrong.
I love you my dear lady.
This I know is true.
I doubt I'll ever love again.
The way that I love you.

I know what is ahead, you see.
A time will come you come to me.
Then a couple we will be.
A loving couple you and me.
We will be two but also one.
A new life we will have begun.

It is now for us to see.
If there should be a you and me.
I think we should so let us see.
Once we see if we should be.
I know to see you makes me smile.
My special lady dressed in style.
I would love for you to smile for me.
It is a pleasure I don't yet know.
I love to see you smile though.
Even though it is not mine.
It makes me smile every time.

If you will now come to me?
So, we can be a happy we.
Because I love you like I do.
There is nothing more that I can do.
Except to tell you I love you.
And pray to God, you love me too.

In a few months it will be.
Time for us to become we.
Time for you to stand and judge.
If you can love what I'm made of.
If you can then we will be.
A happy couple you and me.

Now that you are here with me.
are we two instead of three?
Once it is what we have done.
Two is more than one.
So, you see we are three.
Me and you do make we.

Now dear that I have you here.
My lonesome heart is full of cheer.
Through this darling I can see.
Quite a future there for me.
All I know dear that which was.
Is now a future full of love.

You are so special this I see.
Do you see the same in me?
With you is where I wish to be.
So, tell me now that this can be.
I'll stay with you until the end.
Then wish to do it all again.

I give all my love to you.
I do not know what else to do.
If you love me back? you see.
we are both winners you and me.
but together we must be.
for there to be a you and me.

I could not wait to tell you.
Just the way I feel.
I want you to know for sure.
That my love for you is real.

I know that I love you.
So, it is also true.
I do not want just anyone.
Only you will do.
I just want to spend my life.
Gently holding you.

I just want to be with you.
That is all I want to do.
I want to have you here with me.
Every single day.
I want to wake up next to you.
Then fall asleep that way.

If I could only hold you.
Gently in my arms.
If I could just assure you.
I'd do you no harm.
If you could just give me your love.
We have a gift from up above.
That me and you were meant to be.
A couple we should always be.

I have many pens.
This my dear is true.
I use every one of them.
To write my love for you.
I use them to write down.
All my love for you.
I can't wait till you're in town.
To tell you I love you.

I want to Say I love you.
In some special way.
all I know is I love you.
I hope that is ok.
The words themselves aren't special.
What they mean sure is.
I love you in a special way.
I love you with all my heart.
Forever and a day.

I wish that we could be as one.
You and I have just begun.
Soon together we will be.
A loving couple you and me.
Free to face the world as one.
Together we can't be undone.
But sometimes one and one make three.
Something more than you and me.
We might create a family.

You are always on mind these days.
There is nothing I can do.
You are the one to walk through life with.
This I know is true.
You are the only one I want.
You and only you.
The only thing that's certain.
Is that I love you.
When I saw your picture.
on my computer screen.
I knew I had to have you.
And right here with me.
Your gentle eyes and gorgeous smile.
You stood there all dressed in style.
I could not help but see.
We could build a better life.
One for you and me.

I knew I had to have you.
When I laid eyes on you.
You are oh so beautiful.
I knew not what to do.
I had to tell you how I felt.
I looked at you my heart did melt.
I can't explain the way I felt.
To look at you what do I see?
A better life for you and me.

When I saw you smile?
I said you smiled at me.
Your smile is so lovely.
It gets the best of me.
I want to get to know you.
To bring you in my life.
And with all my hope.
One day you'll be my wife.

I want to write you once again.
To tell you how I feel.
I feel for you a special way.
And that dear one's the deal.
I want you to love me.
More with every day.
And dear one I promise.
To love you in that way.

I fell in love at first sight.
And more with every day.
I hope it does not freak you out.
That I feel this way.
You have a smile so lovely.
It brightens up my day.
The thing that I hope most in life.
Is that you feel this way.

The first time that I looked at you.
I knew just who I saw.
I saw the one that would be mine.
And I knew I would take my time.
To win your heart away.
I look at your photo.
I do it every day.
I knew I had to have you.
This I know is true.
That is because the one want.
Is you and only you.

Please tell me that you want me.
Because I do want you.
I want to make you mine you see.
It is with you I wish to be.
I wish that I could be with you.
Every single day.
That is only If you want me in that way.

Now my darling do you see.
You are the only one for me.
You are the starlight in my sky.
You are the reason for my why.
You bring sweet loving to my life.
I want you to be my wife.
I want to spend my life with you.
That's what I most want to do.
You are the reason for my smile.
I have known this all the while.
You came to me I fell in love.
You're like an angel from above.

Tell me darling do you see.
The man I am that I call me.
That I love you more than me.
You are the reason that I am.
Why I be the best I can.
Any less just will not do.
I must be my best for you.
Tell me I am the man for you.
That no one else will do.
Just tell me I am your man.
You'll make me happy if you can.

On the day I found you.
It was a beautiful beginning.
I knew that you were special.
When you wrote to me.
I also knew that one day you would marry me.
I knew right then you and I were surely meant to be.

I have told you that I love you.
Why because it's true.
Really all I want to do.
Is stay in love with you.
Be careful what you do.
It is not just my heart you will break.
You will also break the one in you.

The thing that I most want to see.
Is the smile you wear for me.
I'll know it when I see you.
If it is from the heart.
I believe it truly is and that's a place to start.
So, wear that special smile that is meant for me.
It is that special smile.
That I long to see.

Know this that I love you.
Please believe it's true.
I don't want just anyone.
Only you will do.
That is because my dear.
I'm deep in love with you.

I know that when you get here.
I want to see your smile.
I'll know by the smile you wear.
If you will stay awhile.
I've tried to win your heart away.
I hope that is ok.
I just want to be your man.
I hope you tell me that I am.

Once I have you by my side.
I will not wonder or ask why.
I'll just try to let you see.
The man inside that I call me.
Make you smile see what I'll do.
I'll dedicate myself to you.

When I can walk through life with you
And watch you smile the way you do.
Just to see you smile at me.
Will warm these eyes when I see.
A lovely smile that's meant for me.

You tell me that I have you.
I believe that it is true.
You are in my life to stay.
I would not want another way.
I tell you that I love you.
Please believe that it is true.
You mean so very much to me.
That it's you I wish to please.

We can have a brand-new start.
If of my life you are a part.
Yes, together we will see.
A brand-new life for you and me.
If you and I are true to heart?
Then my dear we'll never part

I was lonely this is true.
Then good fortune brought me you.
Once you came into my life.
I knew one day you'd be my wife.
If with me, you choose to stay?
I will never walk away.

How I wish that you were here.
So, I could hold you close my dear.
I both want and love you see.
Could it be that you love me?
If you, can I'm glad you do?
For I want no one else but you.

I write you this to tell you dear.
If you still want me? I'm still here.
I still want you bad sweetheart.
One thing I am is true to heart.
I mean what I say my dear.
to that end I'll make it clear.
Yes, my dear I want you here.

On the day that you arrive.
Is the day I'll feel alive.
I just wait for you my dear.
I love you much let me be clear.
I just want to be with you.
There's nothing I would rather do.
Than spend my life in love with you.

You bring me joy.
You make me sing.
I know your love's a splendid thing.
The day you walked into my life.
Content to be my loving wife.
You made me happy I did cheer.
All because I have you here
You're so special it is true.
I'm very much in love with you.

When I look at you, I see.
A lovely lady that's for me.
You make me happy you should know.
A happy road is what we sow.
I still wonder can it be?
That you are in love with me.
The only thing I need from you.
For you to love me like you do.
Know then what you mean to me.
You my dear are everything.

I wait for you, my darling.
You make my poor heart sing.
Because you make me happy.
You get the best of me.
I just didn't know dear.
How much I need you here.
Though we are so far apart.
You are first within my heart.

I write to you often.
In fact, it's every day.
I write you every morning.
I have a lot to say.
I have to say I love you.
I hope you love me too.
I'll just wait to have you here.
That is all that I can do my dear.
I tell you that I love you.
I hope you love me to.

I knew it when I saw you.
Right there from the start.
I knew I when I let you in.
That you would win my heart.
And you surely did that with your written word.
For when I read these words it seems I also herd.
I don't know how that's possible.
you didn't speak a word.
I knew it when I heard you
the circle would complete.
I already Knew that your voice would be sweet.

I tell you that I love you.
And my dear that's true.
I long to see your smiling face.
I long to have you in my space.
I want you with me every day.
I don't want another way.
There are better days ahead.
It is my deepest wish of all.
That someday we will wed.
One day soon yes, I can see.
I'll be a part of more than me.
Half a couple wait and see.
I'll be a part of you and me.
That is what I wish to be.

I am not a shallow man.
The truth is I am who I am.
I can be a strong man though.
I don't always let it show.
Some people see an easy mark.
I'm not a guppy or a shark.
I am a man that's true to heart.
I won't let you down you see.
I can't do that and still be me.

Every time I think of you.
I don't feel sad I don't feel blue.
You are special I can tell.
Myself to you is who I sell.
Is there to be a you and me.
I do wish for there to be.

Perhaps one day we will see.
If you are the one for me.
I wish to know you oh so well.
Will we spark how can I tell.
I wish to spend my time with you.
Tell me I am the one for you.

Tell me you think it should be.
You think that you're the one for me.
that a couple we will be.
that I'm for you and you're for me.
I do believe you are the one.
My life of searching is now done.
Let me be the one for you.
I wish to say that I love you.

I don't know you well just yet.
So, I don't know just what I'll get.
You seem to have a warm soft heart.
If of a couple, we're a part.
I want to know you oh so well.
There is so much that we can tell.
Do you think that it can be?
Can there be a you and me.

I see love within your eyes.
I know you'll never say goodbye.
Now I say to you these words.
So, my love for you is heard.
I won't leave you no not me.
Nor you my dear I won't deceive.
I am so lucky you love me.
You are so great, and I'm just me.

I have loved you for so long.
A love like ours just can't be wrong.
I am so happy I could sing.
Because to me it's love you bring.
I don't know just what to say.
But our loves not just ok.
I will love you all my life.
I am so lucky you're my wife.

Though free time is hard to find.
I'll tell you now, what's on my mind.
I wish to take you out today.
Tell me you will say ok.
What I have to say to you.
Is that I hope you want me too.
I do wish to be with you.
Now tell me that you love me too.

I wish to take you out today.
There are no games I wish to play.
I love to spend my time with you.
You make me happy when I'm blue.
That's why I wish to be with you.
You make me feel the way I do.
I only hope you feel it too.
When I say that I love you.

We've been together for so long.
I knew then it was not wrong.
Although different we may be
A couple we are meant to be.
Now I'm telling this to you.
No one else but you will do.

Although we're not a couple yet.
I now have a running bet.
We'll be together this I know.
I feel for you and let it show.
There is one thing to let you know.
With another I won't go.
That I wish to win your heart.
And of your life become a part.

This I know when I'm with you.
I don't feel sad I don't feel blue.
I always smile when I'm with you.
There's nothing else I'd rather do.
That's because I do love you.
And I hope you love me too.
When I see you, my heart swells?
I've fallen under your sweet spell.
You have a way that makes me see.
How to be a better me.
When I saw you, I could tell?
Once we're together we'll do well.
You seem to see just who I am.
That I do the best I can.
You're quite special this I see.
You seem to see the inner me.
Since you're with me I can see.
Everything I'm meant to be.

I look at you and I can tell.
Upon me you have cast a spell.
When I see you smile at me?
You are everything I need.
Yes, I want you this is true.
I seem to see the inner you.
you seem so close yet far away.
I love you is what I say.
I want to say I love you, in a very, special way.
In fact, I want to tell you each, and every day.
To tell you once is not enough.
It simply will not do.
I've already told you at least a time or two.
I'll express my love as long as I'm with you.
I want you to know that I'm in love with only you.

I'd like to say I love you.
In a special way.
The way that I would tell you.
Would keep the doubts away.
There should not be any doubts.
Not even one.
You will know for certain.
As soon as I am done.
So, I'll say that I love you.
It's simple but it's true
Just to leave no doubts at all.
Darling I love you.

Know this that my love is true.
And that I love only you.
This I wonder can it be.
That it is only you I see.
So, I hope that it is true.
That it is me that's loved by you.

Even though we are apart.
It is you that fills my heart.
Full of hopes and full of dreams.
If it's truly meant to be.
That it really comes to pass.
We will finally be at last.

Can there be a you and me.
Was it truly meant to be?
When I saw you standing there?
It was then you smiled at me.
It made me smile that you could see.
Will you then go out with me?
if you will then you will see.
We my dear are meant to be.

I miss you every day your gone.
Your time at work it seems so long.
I know that you'll come home at night.
When you return its pure delight?

I love the way you make me feel.
All warm and now complete.
You make me feel I'm ten feet tall and built
like superman.
That's because you love me just the way I am.
You are the most of all good things.
That I must admit.
You bring out the best in me.
To make me never quit.
I've always been quite capable.
Of many ample feats.
Now that you are in my life.
My life is now complete.

You're so special this is true.
I want no one say for you.
You make me think of who I am.
You make me feel I am a man.
If you love me say it's true.
I'll reply that I love you.

You're not with me here today.
You are at work and that's ok..
I'll be here when you get home.
Then I will not be alone.
Then my dear you'll be at home.

I've looked for you a lifetime.
I finally found you here.
I knew it when I saw you.
That it was you my dear.
You're everything I wanted.
Everything I need.
I knew when I first saw you.
God gave you to me.
I knew that I would love you.
It took no time at all.
I'll say now that I love you.
That my dear's my call.

I knew that I was here for you.
And you were here for me.
I have one question for you.
This was meant to be.
The only question that I have.
Will you come with me?

I would like to tell you.
Just the way I feel.
I'd like to find a special way.
But hear my dear's the deal.
I want to say I love you.
I'll try to keep it real.
I love you more than words can say.
I only hope that is ok.
I couldn't find another way.
Except to say I love you.
More with every day.

I knew it when I saw you here.
It was to my good fortune.
I knew it by the smile you wore.
It was by fate I chose your store.
I came today to talk to you.
To ask you out to dinner.
That if you will go out with me.
That I'm the lucky winner.
When I saw you standing there?
Lovely smile and pretty hair.
That I would ask you out with me.
I know how lucky I would be.
If only you'd go out with me?

CPSIA information can be obtained
at www.ICGtesting.com
Printed in the USA
LVHW032026220222
711655LV00004B/109